COME T[...]
LAWYERS WHO ARE . . .

Sensitive

"Please be advised that we were unable to obtain a defense verdict in the case. As a result, pending appeal, it appears that you will be liable for $150,000 in general damages. We hope that your recent heart surgery was a success."

Compassionate

"We are pleased to advise you that since our last correspondence, the plaintiff has died; therefore, we will be proceeding with our Motion to Dismiss."

Upholders of Truth

"We had hoped that plaintiff's deposition testimony would be vague and unclear. Unfortunately, he knew what he was talking about."

Worth Every Penny Charged

"Since we do not wish to arouse any interest on the part of the plaintiff, I would recommend that we continue to do what we have been doing, which is nothing. Enclosed, please find our current bill."

LAWYERS
SAY
THE
DARNDEST
THINGS

Steve Kluger

IVY BOOKS • NEW YORK

Ivy Books
Published by Ballantine Books
Copyright © 1990 by Steve Kluger

Library of Congress Catalog Card Number: 90-92926

ISBN - 0-8041-0558-8

Manufactured in the United States of America

First Edition: June 1990

Dedicated to
JOHN J. COSTANZO, ESQ.
(1924—1985)
who said,
"Jesus H. Christ—
whatever you do,
don't write a book."

AUTHOR'S NOTE

Although, by definition, I am a published novelist and journalist, as well as a produced playwright, these statistics are impressive only to my own family. All it really means is that I don't make any money. For this reason, it usually becomes necessary to seek some sort of temporary employment in the real world long about the time the MasterCard bill comes in. However, waiting tables is definitely not my metier, there is a sixty-three-year-old woman in Beverly Hills wearing a spinach souffle who can tell you why, nor is tending a deli counter, as anyone who has ever attempted to distinguish between cream cheese and lard will likewise explain. Driving a cab posed a unique challenge—briefly—less for me than for the eighteen gas pumps in the greater Los Angeles area that I inadvertently flattened while maneuvering the way I imagined de Niro would; and gunrunning for the Cosa Nostra never even got off the ground when it was pointed out that this is not something you seriously consider when you're a short Jew. Finally, a buddy pulled me aside and said, "Look—you're a writer. Can't you at least type?"

(Well, yeah. Eighty-one words a minute. With four fingers.)

That is how I wound up in the word processing departments of some of the largest law firms in Southern California. It's been eight years. But it's only temporary. I swear to God!

Steve Kluger
Los Angeles
September 1987

P.S. One other thing. Every word in this book is legit. I mean, it would have to be. Nobody could make this stuff up.

"DEAR CLIENT"

We had hoped that plaintiff's deposition testimony would be vague and unclear. Unfortunately, he knew what he was talking about.

I have been assigned to the further handling of this claim, and can assure you of my abilities in this regard. Please contact me if you has any questions.

Inasmuch as your client is ninety-seven years old, we strongly suggest that his deposition be scheduled for the week after next.

Plaintiff has a tenth-grade education, does not wear glasses, and has never been convicted of a felony.

Please be advised that we were unable to obtain a defense verdict in this case. As a result, pending appeal, it appears that you will be liable for $150,000 in general damages. We hope that your recent heart surgery was a success.

Plaintiff's health was good, the doors and windows were clean.

The witness appeared at his deposition neatly attired in spectacles.

It appears that we will have a difficult time obtaining a defense verdict if this case is tried before a live jury.

The deponent has been convicted of several felonies, and has served time in prison for grand theft auto somewhere in the Midwest. He should make a better-than-average witness on his own behalf at time of trial.

Based upon the answers to interrogatories, our subsequent investigation, and a review of the pertinent medical records, it is our considered opinion that we will be able to nail plaintiff to the wall.

Considering that the plaintiff is of an advanced age and in poor health, we would recommend prolonging any discovery for as long as possible.

In attempting to set the witness' deposition, we discovered that he has died. We had thought he was in Jamaica.

If you have any other questions or appearances to be made on this case, please ask somebody else.

We refer you to the attached Exhibit D, which is attached hereto thereat herein.

We are pleased to advise you that since our last correspondence, the plaintiff has died; therefore, we will be proceeding with our Motion to Dismiss.

Plaintiff is a twenty-six-year-old South American who has never worn glasses.

Since we do not wish to arouse any interest on the part of the plaintiff, I would recommend that we continue to do what we have been doing, which is nothing. Enclosed, please find our current bill.

Incidentally, I happened to be looking through our closet and ran across a briefcase that had a surprising number of things bearing your name, including a bottle of suspicious-looking pills. I wonder if you have managed to miss a small briefcase, or if this is just a gift to our good firm from your good firm.

The deponent testified in a sincere and straightforward manner, although most of his testimony was made up by his attorney.

Please be advised that the documents you requested in your Motion to Compel do not exist. As such, we do not have them. Furthermore, if we did have them, we would not give them to you.

Please advise if plaintiff has any other elated claims.

We are refraining from providing you with copies of the medical records, which are enclosed.

Originally the deponent had wanted to become a doctor, until she viewed some motion pictures in high school on how the human body works. Now she wants to be a stenographer.

The deponent was dressed in a very expensive co-ordinated outfit that I hope she wears to trial.

Dr. Herbert is an attractive, handsome, articulate man, although he did not testify to these facts.

Please allow us to clear up the discrepancy. Although it was the plaintiff who was operated on and who is suing for medical malpractice, her husband is the one who died. He had nothing to do with it.

It was before her death that the decedent became pregnant.

Mr. Simpson stated that he was jostled about the inside of the cab, which, as you know, is enclosed.

LAWYERS SAY THE DARNDEST THINGS

Please find attached a carbon copy of one of our experts.

Please date this letter accordingly. Actually, you can date it whenever you want. It's a year and a half late anyway.

Our expert came to his deposition dressed in leotards. He will make a good impression on a jury should this matter proceed to trial.

I am enclosing copies of two reports which I hereto refer to in attempt to respond to the pleadings attached to the file.

Mrs. Williams weighed approximately 250 pounds and was referred to a Dr. Stout.

Enclosed is our current status report on this matter. Please be advised that this case is a mess.

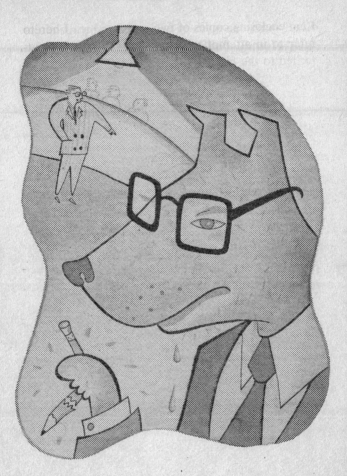

By way of further handling, I would recommend that someone harness the plaintiff's attorney and send him to obedience school.

Kindly advise us as to how you wish to handle plaintiff's attorney. Evidently, screaming doesn't help.

I recommend that we settle this matter as soon as possible before the plaintiff realizes how guilty we really are.

Deponent spoke with a heavy foreign accent, rather a Mexican accent, which is not foreign in California.

Please notify us immediately if you do not receive this letter.

We have successfully managed to locate plaintiff, although we still do not know where he is.

Plaintiff is suffering from shortness of breath, blurred vision, and insomnia. In 1983, he tar papered the roof of his house.

We were not informed in advance of the deposition that the plaintiff only speaks Japanese. As a result, nobody understood a word he was saying.

I would normally recommend a minimal settlement to dispose of this matter; however, considering that our machine did, in fact, kill the decedent, I wouldn't imagine we had much of a chance.

By way of further preparation, we will take the deposition of the plaintiff if we can find him. If we can't, we won't.

Plaintiff filed his Complaint in January and then disappeared. I suggest that we not try to find him.

Mr. Reiner's dry-cleaning business is located in Lake Tahoe, where it is called Mr. Reiner's Dry-Cleaning Business. I think.

Co-defendant, in fact, is not a prostitute but a real-estate agent.

Gentlemen: This is to advise you that nothing has happened on this matter since our last correspondence to you. If something *should* happen on this matter, we will of course advise you of same. If you have any questions about this, please contact me.

The witness appeared for her deposition smartly attired in a business suit. She is articulate and casually black.

Deponent began to testify that he may have been partially responsible for the accident, but changed his mind when his attorney kicked him under the table.

The weather was clear, the sun was shining. It was daylight outside.

Cross-complainant's counsel has tentatively set the deposition for some time in late May or early June. Please advise me if you are available on that date.

Plaintiff complained of various achenesses and stiff-nesses.

Although I only sat in for part of the deposition, I can assure you that everything we have heard about this witness is true. He's a real pip.

Plaintiff states it is her belief that her neck injuries were caused by a jerk.

As to what plaintiffs will claim for future loss of earnings, we can only imaginate.

I enclose copies of the Cadillac involved in the accident.

If pressed for a defense, I am sure we could find something in the *Code of Civil Procedure*, which prohibits just about everything.

Plaintiff Nancy MacGregor appeared at her deposition casually attired in a maroon sweater and skirt. She is five feet, six inches tall, with light brown hair, a ruddy complexion, and a square jaw that makes her look somewhat like Charlton Heston.

Plaintiff was discharged in August 1977 for having sex with an immediate subordinate. He had originally been hired under an oral contract.

Plaintiff's expert, Mr. Preston, had only been in a brewery three times before being retained in this case as a tourist.

Four thousand dollars has been paid for funeral expenses for the motorcycle.

Although plaintiff did, in fact, suffer the accidental amputation of the four fingers of his major hand, we nevertheless believe that his claimed damages are far in excess of that injury. After all, he still has a thumb.

Plaintiff states that she is presently suffering from a lack of sphincter control in her left hand.

Mr. Kallman appears to be forty-five years old, with dirty black hair, red eyes, and grease-smeared clothing. He comes across as being quite crazy and would therefore make only an average witness.

She appeared for her deposition wearing a blue sweater dress. She is slightly overweight and the dress was slightly too small.

Plaintiff weighs one hundred and twenty-five pounds with a driver's license.

Deponent would make an excellent impression on a jury at time of trial and so it is unfortunate that she has nothing to say.

ROAD
SAFETY

The bus operator claims he ran over the plaintiff because he was behind schedule.

The decedent was killed when he ran a red light traveling west on Pico Boulevard.

The plaintiff's vehicle was being driven by his deceased wife.

The plaintiff stated that she had never ridden that particular bus operator before.

Plaintiff stated that the vehicle does not operate its brake in normal, except manual.

By virtue of the fact that your assured was driving the subject vehicle without any brakes, in an intoxicated state, and well over the posted speed limit, there would appear to be some liability on our part.

The vehicle involved in the accident partially left the roadway, straddled the curb bordering the street, hit a newspaper storage bin, and eventually struck a concrete light bulb.

LAWYERS SAY THE DARNDEST THINGS

Please state at what rate of speed you were traveling in the vicinity of the question.

Plaintiff stated that he usually does not operate his vehicle inebriated, except sometimes.

This is to request that you postpone your inspection of our vehicle, inasmuch as we cannot seem to find the bus.

Plaintiff's vehicle continued in the number two lane while traveling in the number one lane.

Plaintiff stated that the collision involved bus number
7018. We claim that bus number 7018 does not exist.
If, in fact, bus number 7018 does not exist, plaintiff
might have a difficult time proving that he collided
with it.

From what we have been able to ascertain, the bus
operator involved in this accident was a white male,
approximately four years old.

They inquired into the plaintiff's health and he told
them that he was fine but his car was not.

MEDICAL
FOUL
PRACTICE

The deponent stated that she became pregnant during the subject surgery.

Plaintiff claims that he underwent a hysterectomy shortly thereafter.

It appears that all surgery was adequately performed—up until the time the patient died.

The physician recommended calf-raising as a remedy.

During the operation, the insured inadvertently punctuated the plaintiff's abdominal wall.

Plaintiff was administered Dilantin shortly after he died.

Plaintiff was admitted to the hospital for a colostomy, during the course of which a section of his semi-colon was removed.

Plaintiff is claiming damages far above what we suspect she actually incurred as a result of the silicone implants. Therefore, this appears to be another one of your inflatable breast cases.

Plaintiff is claiming $125,000 in medical specials, which we believe is grossly exaggerated. If he will not submit to a medical examination, we would recommend an autopsy.

Plaintiff was asked if he had had his teeth cleaned recently, then was administered penicillin immediately and rushed to the hospital.

Plaintiff is alleging medical foul practice.

Despite the extent of plaintiff's injuries, the doctor did not take her out and shoot her.

The doctor sent the patient home by using a cane.

Although the patient was unhappy, the doctor indicated that he intended to follow her and keep her as content as possible.

Plaintiff claims that she must have become pregnant on the day of her wedding. This was confirmed by a pregnancy test sixty-eight weeks later.

Plaintiff's claim against the hospital is that her husband was defective when he got out.

All medical bills were attached to the plaintiff.

Deponent states that she told the doctor of her injury to her head and was thereafter referred to a urologist.

Once he was treated at the hospital, his hand was placed in a bowel with a cold saline solution.

Our liability stems from the fact that apparently the left knee surgery was performed on the right knee.

LAWYERS SAY THE DARNDEST THINGS

The incision was made with a surgical scaffold.

The plaintiff states that she had a tubal litigation.

On March 29, 1982, the patient complained of intense pain in her right shoulder, for which she was injected into Dr. Wallace.

WHAT
I
REALLY
MEANT
WAS . . .

Plaintiff lives alone with her husband.

We initially prepared a demand for jury, which jury was summarily executed.

Plaintiff's injuries were caused by an alleged washing machine.

47

These conclusions were drawn during a recent conversation with myself.

Plaintiff died two weeks after the subject accident, and hence will not be available for deposition.

Please find enclosed copies of the plaintiff.

Plaintiff has a two-year-old daughter who is presently unemployed.

Deponent advised us that plaintiff's counsel was purchased in October of 1978.

The tank itself was filled with gasoline, aviation fuel, and the plaintiff.

Further, prior to the accident of November 3, Mr. Costello was actively involved in dog training with his wife; however, he indicated that those activities have been discontinued and that his sexual activities have been limited.

It was determined by the tire company's investigators that the airline accident was caused by witchcraft.

The incident occurred when a boat fell out of the vending machine.

This will be a Motion to Compel. We are attorneys for the comma.

Plaintiff appeared to be his stated age of thirty-seven, and is a black male Caucasian.

The plaintiff's wife's name is Cynthia and his daughter's name is Kim. They have no children.

Once plaintiffs arrived, they met their friends and sat on a campfire and talked and joked.

The deposition began at 10:00, although the deponent did not arrive until 11:30.

He has a seven-year-old son who resides in Sacramento with his wife.

They are the liability carrier for your daughter, the insurance company.

The deponent stated that she spent the night with a friend who wasn't there.

This is to advise you that your presence was not required at the Arbitration Conference which was not held last week.

He then stated he bit into a piece of veal which was not a piece of veal.

He later brought the car to the baggage area, where the bags and his wife were loaded into the car.

Plaintiff proceeded to walk up the hill. On foot.

We requested that the trial in this matter be held in the early fall. The judge concurred and set a date of April 6th.

Please advise if you wish us to utilize in-house experts or out-house experts.

All bus operators are required to inspect and satisfy themselves.

Mrs. Delaney's leg was implanted in Dr. Bell's opinion.

It is our opinion that plaintiff's mind is a terrible stretch of roadway.

Plaintiff possesses sandy brown hair and an Arizona driver's license.

By appointment, they met at the plaintiff's son's house, which is near Mr. Stewart's house. The meeting lasted about one-half hour and they talked mainly about tacos.

The plaintiff was alive at the time he filed the action.

The decedent was admitted to the Southland Urological Church.

The vehicle was purchased by the son but owned by Mr. Cowles, the adopted father for insurance purposes.

Mr. Doakes, a technician, made appropriate adjustments to the plaintiff.

Mr. Daily attended his deposition dressed.

It is alleged that, on said date, plaintiff's decedent was operating a 1978 automobile when she experienced a deflation of her right rear.

The patient at this time was referred to a gentle dentist for further evaluation.

He suffered a fracture to his left foreman.

The patient was found on the floor in the nurse.

During the breast surgery, plaintiff received several memory implants.

Plaintiff claims that she was rear-hyphened by defendant.

Defendants pointed out that Mrs. Walker had escaped from Frontera Prison through the use of her deposition testimony.

If you mail a formal request, along with a $7.00 fee, to the Registrar-Recorder, you can receive a copy of your Death Certificate within fifteen days.

Ms. Pelsky was not looking at the ground, although she knew it was there.

She advised him that it was her and that she was there. He seemed very surprised by that fact.

Plaintiff's attorney advised me that he recently passed away.

Deponent was friendly with an accent.

She wears glasses for nearsightedness that are sharp and witty.

MOVING
PAPERS

The defendant objects to this interrogatory on the grounds that it is more appropriate to a *Code of Civil Procedure* Section 2037 demand. However, in the spirit of liberal discovery, and without waiving said objection, and in reserving all rights, defendant responds that it does not know.

If any injury or damage was suffered by the plaintiff, the same was proximately caused by the plaintiff in failing to use the subject toilet seat in a reasonably foreseeable manner.

I declare that I am an attorney licensed to practice
law before all the courts of the State of California,
and an ass with the above-mentioned law firm.

I don't care, under penalty of perjury, that the fore-
going is true and correct.

Were you ever imprisoned? If so, please state:
   (a) Whether or not you served your term;
   (b) Whether or not you escaped. If so, please give
      the date of your escape and the method em-
      ployed (i.e., at gunpoint or incognito, etc.)

If any injury or damage was suffered by the plaintiff, the same was proximately caused and contributed to by the plaintiff in failing to use the subject spaghetti in a reasonably foreseeable manner.

Please state all the injuries to the subject head and its component parts.

Answering paragraphs 18 and 31 of the Complaint, these defendants refer to the paragraphs referenced therein and incorporate these defendants' answers thereto herein by reference.

If the whereabouts of the subject document are un-known, please state where it can be located.

Please state whether you have suffered from any other lover ailments.

"You" means all persons employed by your company, whether real or artificial.

If any injury or damage was suffered by the plaintiff, the same was proximately caused and contributed to by plaintiff in failing to use the subject heart valve in a reasonably foreseeable manner.

I am an attorney licensed to practice law before all of the states in California.

"This Code section was implemented to further the expedition of the court's calendar, and to insure that justice would not proceed blindly." *American Optical Association v. Superior Court.*

The court, in its discretion, is permitted to strike irrelevant, redundant, and redundant matters.

At all times mentioned herein, January 21, 1978, was a public street in the County of Los Angeles, State of California.

Discovery is continuing, and this defendant reserves the right to introduce sexually discovered evidence at time of trial.

I am the counsel of record for the named partiers.

If called upon as a witness, I could and would competently do so. This Declaration is executed this 32nd day of June, 1983.

That case is totally distinguishable from the instant case as there the Trial Court after nine days determined that only five days would be permitted to give the plaintiff two days to present his case for a total of eleven days, allowing the defendant three days, as opposed to the two days of plaintiff. The court was quite clear on this point.

Objection. This interrogatory is vague, ambiguous, unintelligible, and not reasonably calculated to lead to the discovery of admissible evidence. However, without waiving said objection, and in the spirit of liberal discovery, defendant replies, "Maybe."

If the plaintiff has suffered or sustained any damage or injury as alleged in the Complaint, the same was proximately caused and contributed to by the plaintiff in failing to use the subject tree in a reasonably foreseeable manner.

Have you ever suffered a loss of smell in either ear?

If your answer to the preceding interrogatory is in the affirmative, state whether or not such loss of smell was rectified by the use of a hearing aid.

Have you ever suffered a *partial* loss of smell in either ear? If so, state how long a period of time before you were able to smell fully again, and out of which ear.

We need to know the number of cigarettes the witness smoked in response to interrogatory No. 18.

HAVE
YOU
EVER
SEEN
A
PEANUT
STAND?

What is the current address of the subject swimming pool?

The officer, in his deposition, stated that at the time of the accident, an inebriation test was performed on the subject van.

The gunshot was apparently filed by a member of the Sheriff's Department.

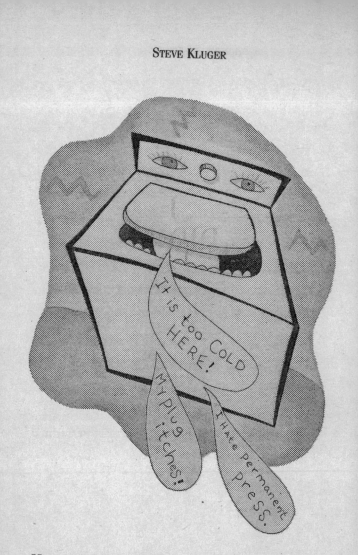

Have you ever received any complaints from the subject appliance?

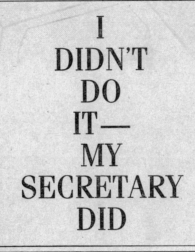

I
DIDN'T
DO
IT—
MY
SECRETARY
DID

I recently contacted Mrs. Mary Webber of Baker and Baker, who ate the client's bankruptcy attorneys.

Plaintiff was formerly employed as a crook, but is presently out of work.

Please state the name, address and telephone number of the piece of wood that struck plaintiff.

If you have any questions, please hesitate to contact me.

We took the plaintiff's deposition and apostrophe.

Mal Practice Claims
2136 Third Street
Los Angeles, California

Dear Mr. Practice:

LAWYERS SAY THE DARNDEST THINGS

The deponent presently resides in Hermosa Peach.

The deposition of the cross-defendant was taken under our offices.

The deposition continued after a forty-five minute lynch break.

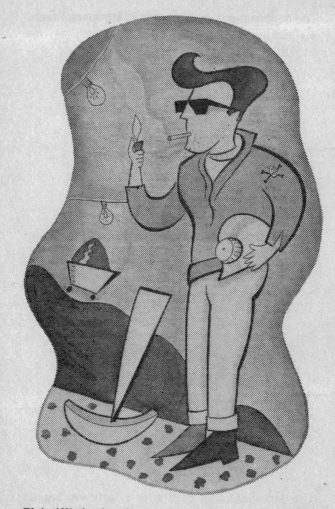

Plaintiff's husband was employed as a cool miner.

LAWYERS SAY THE DARNDEST THINGS

On the above date, I appeared in Department G for the hearing on the interlocutory judgment on the disillusion of marriage.

There were still people drinking and eating the Lafayette Room.

Please see the objection as preciously asserted above.

The sympathy factor should weigh heavily, inasmuch as the decedent left behind an attractive window and two children.

The undersigned would be available to mate with and consult with plaintiff's counsel, regarding any of the above matters discussed.

Total medicals come to $3,640, with funeral expenses of $11.95.

Mr. Norton came to his deposition in a casual dress.

As to the injuries suffered, plaintiff states that she has lost ass sensation in her arms.

Thank you for your assistance in the handling of this matter. I was a pleasure working with you.

The court ordered defendant's Motion off calendar, due to a typographical errof in the Amended Notice of Continuance.

Please attack the chart which I have clipped to the correspondence file.

Mr. Strattner advised that the Wisconsin federal court has not yet ruled on any of the morons for summary judgment.

Please state the number of weakly sexual relations.

Mr. Golden is a twenty-five-year-old black man. He came to his deposition rather casually dressed. He has medium brown hair and a rather scraggly bear.

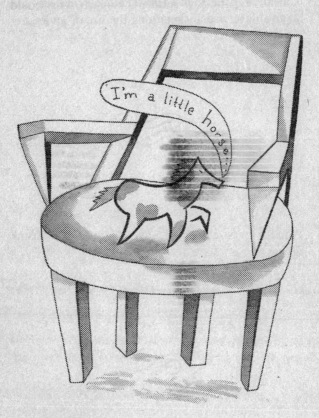

Plaintiff complains of a persistent sore throat and difficulty swallowing. At her deposition, she also claimed to be a little horse.

Currently, plaintiff has a bowel movement every four to five days, usually requiring the use of an enemy.

Plaintiff was convicted several times for drunk diving.

Plaintiffs herein pray for damage$ as follows:

Deponent is a Board-certified sturgeon.

Please review the enclosed interrogatories, and then sing them.

Plaintiff lived at Carpeteria for five years.

PLEASE
TELL
THE COURT,
IN
YOUR
OWN
WORDS . . .

Plaintiff stated that she has been married seven times. We obtained the names and addresses of her former spouses, except for a Mr. Harper, whose first name she could not recall.

This eighty-nine-year-old plaintiff claims that as a result of the accident, she can no longer dance.

The deponent stated that at the time of the incident alleged, her husband was an electrician/gynecologist.

The plaintiff was a supervisor at the plant and was reportedly hated by his employees because he made them work.

The deponent stated, "I was sitting behind the bush and I saw something move, so I raised my rifle and shot the plaintiff because I thought he was a turkey."

Plaintiff complained that she suffered mental injury to her leg.

Plaintiff stated that when he found out all of his belongings had been sold, he cried a lot.

The plaintiff said his neck and body were thrown back and forth striking his back and the back of his neck against the seat back.

Plaintiff claims that due to the injury to her left hand, she is having great difficulty walking.

At that time, plaintiff was a general laborer, and did what they call "hang weenies." He was injured when the weenie house exploded, and said it was "raining weenies."

Plaintiff stated that the last time he had sexual relations with the deceased was before she died.

Plaintiff admits that he was inebriated at the time of the incident, but claims he would have made the unsafe lane change even if he had been sober.

The deponent was born in Malaysia in 1942, where she lived for fifteen years before moving to Singapore, Kyoto, and Long Beach.

"I then called the doctor, and he asked me to call him and advise him as to whether or not he should burn all of his records in the different attorneys' offices. The reason he stated was Nixon was stupid in not burning his records and he didn't want to be as stupid as Nixon."

The plaintiff further contends that he has discomfort and that he cannot sit down and stand up at the same time.

He received a telephone call in the middle of the night from some friends who told him that his brother had been in an automobile accident. At first he thought it was a ruse to get him to come to a party.

She advised us that before she met her current husband, she had never seen him before.

Plaintiff claims that the hospital was negligent in its care for the plaintiff, that the decedent's condition was incorrectly diagnosed, that the surgery was inadequately performed, and that improper precautions were taken to avoid internal bleeding. Other than that, she had no complaints about the hospital.

Plaintiff's activities were restricted, including jogging, walking and tennis, although she did not play tennis before the accident.

The stewardess said that there was no problem because the plane could land on one engine. A few minutes later, she talked with the pilot and said nothing but screamed.

The deponent stated that the plaintiff appeared very shaken after the accident. Her face was frightful.

As to the injuries claimed, plaintiff states that, since the accident, whenever she holds her arm straight above her head for more than thirty minutes, her hand becomes numb.

The plaintiff states that she is presently 5½ inches in height, which is approximately ¼ inch shorter than she was at the time of the accident.

Regarding ongoing medical specials, plaintiff indicates in her answers to interrogatories that she can no longer stand up in the backseat of her car.

She claims that she does drink beer, but always stops when she starts getting sick.

"When I found out the plane was going to crash, I put my head between my legs while I looked out the window."

Mr. Porter is alleging fraudulent representation, in that the defendant claimed he was God.

A man arrived in the emergency room and proceeded immediately to the Intensive Care Unit. The deponent assumed the man was a doctor because he was wearing a golf outfit.

Deponent states that she is a sorceress. Her specials include medicals and lost sorcery fees.

Plaintiff Sheba Caplan claims that her marital diffi-culties ended when her husband died.

Plaintiff states that he is his wife's eldest son. I find this unusual.

Plaintiff's soft-tissue injuries were not what initially prompted him to file this lawsuit. He claims he got the idea from the newspaper.

Deponent states that he had intended to marry the decedent after she had recuperated from the surgery. Since she died, however, they did not.

Plaintiff accepted a post with the U.S. Air Force, then gave it up three months later because he was afraid of flying.

Deponent did not speak English very well, which made his testimony difficult to understand. He stated that he began working for his current employer the month that they give out turkeys.

Although plaintiff has never been employed, he is seeking damages for future loss of earnings because he claims that sooner or later he would have.

Mrs. Shaw states that she has many fond remembrances of her father. Yet, when pressed, the only one she could recall was the time he gave her a lawnmower.

On her claim for loss of consortium, she has not made any calculation of the dollar value for her husband's lost services, nor has she any estimate as to what cost she has incurred to have others perform these services.

"Although I am Board-certified in neurosurgery and have probably read the statistics involved, they never stayed in my cerebrum."

Plaintiff states that immediately prior to the accident she turned into a shopping center. This evidently was a mistake. She had intended to turn into a gas station.

"My car was struck by an off-duty police officer who was a sportscar."

"I have had three similar accidents over the past five years, all of them taking place in airport waiting rooms. This is not intentional."

"I knew that plaintiff was going to hit my car the minute I saw her Colorado license plates."

"The last time I was in a car accident, the other driver was backing up and hit my broad side."

Plaintiff stated that he quit his job in September of 1984 because he was tired of demonstrating refrigerators.

The witness claimed that he remembered the day of the accident very well because shortly before the accident he saw a naked man walking down Wilshire Boulevard and he had never seen a naked man on Wilshire Boulevard before.

The plaintiff states that he was home watching television when the fire occurred and that he first smelled smoke during a McDonald's commercial.

Plaintiff claims that Mr. Shelby was negligent in failing to signal before he plowed into her rear end.

Since his retirement, Mr. Ellis enjoyed managing his investments, reading, research, golfing, and keeping his wife happy.

They could not park the ambulance closer to the door, because then they would be blocking the doctors' view of the trees from their dining room.

ABOUT THE AUTHOR

STEVE KLUGER is a left-handed fastballer for the Chicago Cubs until the alarm clock goes off. A former actor whose career on network television began and ended when he played a chicken on "Diff'rent Strokes", he is the author of the novel CHANGING PITCHES, the stage plays BULLPEN, CAFE 50'S, and PILOTS OF THE PURPLE TWILIGHT, and the forthcoming feature films OVER MY DEAD BODY, ALMOST LIKE BEING IN LOVE, and THE TIME OF OUR LIVES. He is a native of Baltimore who was raised in New York and lives in Los Angeles where he roots for the Boston Red Sox. At present, he does not have a lawyer. It is doubtful now that he ever will.